SOUTHALL
and
NORWOOD

A Portrait in Old Picture Postcards

by
William J. Drinkwater

S.B. Publications
1992

CONTENTS

CONTENTS

CONTENTS

S.B. Publications.

Front Cover: Southall Station. c.1905

ACKNOWLEDGEMENTS

The author wishes to thank the following who helped towards the compiling of this book – Ealing Local History Library (for provision of map copies), Southall Library (for provision of information), Miss. E. Barnett (for loan of photographs), Mr. A. Meads (for loan of photographs) Mr. S.C. Flavin (for attending postcard fairs on my behalf), The Southall Chamber of Commerce (for information), together with the local churches, organisations and individuals (each of which have offered help and advice).
    Also Ordnance Survey for permission to reproduce from the Ordnance Survey maps of Southall/Norwood 1894/6 and 1914, and local newspapers for use of their columns and old pictures.
    Especially to Mr. Marcus Taylor (for locating old negatives and producing prints).

THE AUTHOR

William J. Drinkwater was born and bred in Southall in 1914, and lived with his parents at 61 Hartington Road (next door to the Gardiner family involved in the Peasenhall case) for 30 years. Educated at Featherstone Road Boys' School, he experienced the lean years of the 'twenties and thirties' with frequent spells of unemployment.

At the outbreak of the Second World War he joined the Casualty Services in Southall, and saw action as a stretcher party leader, until finally being called up for army service in 1942 with the Royal Army Medical Corps.

When drafted abroad the following year, Bill found himself attached to the British Military Administration in the Dodecanese Islands, and was present at the capitulation of the German Garrison in the Eastern Aegean on 8 May 1945.

On demobilisation, he carved himself a career in building and joinery administration with wide experience in management, surveying, costing and estimating until his retirement in 1978.

For the past thirteen years he has opened up a latent talent of freelance writing, having had short stories broadcast on Radio Bristol. A prolific writer of magazine articles, his interests have found themselves in print regularly in the fields of picture postcard collecting, cigarette card collecting, family history, local history and military history.

Bill – married with a grown-up family – an advanced arthritic, is active in the area of disablement, serving on many committees in North Wiltshire where he now lives.

PREFACE

The Southall/Norwood District was but a rural area until the coming of the railway in 1839, with isolated farmhouses and cottages, surrounded by brick-fields and a canal system which virtually made an island of the place. Any expansion worth mentioning came towards the end of the 19th century, when the early photographer came on the scene to record – mainly on picture postcards – the wonderful and palmy days, when old buildings of character and tranquil village life could be captured for future generations.

The author has aimed to present a period, in text and illustration, from the time the Drinkwater family first set foot on Southall soil around 1885, until its members started to move to fresh fields and pastures new during the Second World War and the coming of the nuclear age of family life.

The book, therefore, tells the story of growth and change as seen through the eyes of one family which saw the place grow over half a century from a population in 1890 of 7,300 people, to one of 8,500 a decade later, 25,000 by 1920, 29,000 in 1930 and 52,000 by the outbreak of WWII. Since then the immigrant influx has increased tremendously that figure, and old Southall families are in the minority.

Little wonder then, that this extreme growth has obliterated most of the Southall which the Drinkwater's knew; its cinemas have gone; its gas works – so important at the turn of the century when it made its own supply – has gone and been replaced by North Sea vintage; but thankfully, the Manor House still remains standing, preserved by the tenancy of the Chamber of Commerce.

However, the greater the change, the greater the interest in things of yesteryear . . . in what things used to be like in the world that has passed in the mist of time. Nothing brings back memories of the days of yore, and reveals the transformations that Southall/Norwood has undergone, as well as old photographs. It is hoped that this collection will appease the appetites of older residents, satisfy the curiosity of many new ones – especially those that come from foreign lands – and encourage further research by others.

None of those who know the area today, or knew it in days past, cannot one feels, but be fascinated by the array of nostalgia presented between the covers of this book.

INTRODUCTION

Southall/Norwood: In the beginning

It requires more than a lively imagination – especially with the late 20th century pulsating cosmopolitan atmosphere of Southall – to go back in time to 5000 BC when practically the whole of Middlesex was covered with trees, scrub and bushland, and wild animals were hunted and killed in order that our forbears might exist.

Only as recently as 1887 evidence of Stone Age human activity in the area was found when excavations were being carried out for a drainage scheme in Norwood Lane (now Tentelow Lane). On that occasion the men engaged in the work unearthed some mammoth bones, a flint spearhead and other flint implements. Likewise, Bronze Age findings of vessels, weapons, implements, moulds and ingots were made at North Hyde which can be seen in the British Museum.

Early Records

As far as can be ascertained the first recorded reference to the area comes from a priest named Werhard. In his will dated AD 830 Werhard left much land to his next of kin, Archbishop Wulfred of Canterbury, in Hayes and Norwood. By this act the Manors of Norwood and Southall came under the Church of Canterbury, so we note famous names appearing as lords of the manor – Dunstan (950-88); Stigand (1052-70); Lefranc (1070-93); Thomas à Becket (1162-70); Stephen Langton (1207-28); Henry Chicheley (1414-43); who did much for St Mary's, Norwood Green and Thomas Cranmer (1533-48).

In the Domesday Survey of 1086 Norwood is included in Hayes (then known as Hesa). Norwood, North Hyde, Northcote, Northolt were all Manor, with Southall Green and Dormandswell classed as being in 'the West Middle Sax' region. The history of the Manor Lands is far from clear. The first Manor of Southall may have been in the Waxlow area, although it is possibly just a farm and not an actual manor, as is evident by the existence of a Waxlow Manor Farm until 1928 after which the Waxlow Estate was built on the land.

Deorman or Deormund (closely associated with William I) was the owner of extensive property, and it is thought that he leased land from his friend, Archbishop Anselm-hence Dormandswell. First records of what was to be Dormandswells House appears in 1382. The modern Dormers Wells dates only from 1863.

In 1383 the manor was sub-let to Stephen Yedding by John Shoredyche for ten years at £22 per annum. During the next 126 years it changed tenants on several occasions and, in 1510, Robert Shoredyche surrendered Dormandwells, a mill and some land to Robert Cheeseman who was then living there. By the time the latter died in 1547 Dormandswells was large enough to have a Chapel.

Cheeseman left the house to his second wife, Alice, who was the daughter of Henry Dacres, a Merchant Taylor. Alice, in turn, left it to her daughter Anne and her husband Francis Chamberlayne, in 1558. In 1578 the Manor was sold to the 10th Baron Dacre, who before his death in 1594 had commenced the building of a manor house *The Wrenns* in Southall Green. As Lady Dacre only survived her husband by eight months, the place was sold by the executors in 1602 and came into the possession of Francis Awsiter who at the same time purchased the Manor of Norwood.

It is on record that Henry VIII used to visit Dormandswells House around 1515 to take part in wild boar hunting across country to Syon House, the home of the Duke of Northumberland. This connects with another very old house, *The Romans*, which stood on the right side of Southall Green where, it is said, Cardinal Wolsey used to stay whilst the King was visiting Dormandswells. (The author, incidentally, lived in *The Romans* in 1920 – at the age of five years – for a short period when his father was steward of the *Old Comrades Association*). Sadly the place was pulled down in the early 'thirties to make way for a parade of shops.

On the death of Lady Dacre her estate at Dormandswells should have gone to her sister's husband, Sampson Leonard, but money problems led to the place falling into ruin and it was eventually pulled down, the site being to the rear of what was Dormers Wells Farm.

The 'well' connection comes from a Chalybeate Water spring which had an iron content and was said to have beneficial properties. The mineral content in the underground waters at times makes itself obvious in the land. Indeed, until quite recent years, the area pools were a fine source of watercress production.

The Manor has always been the proudest historical possession of Southall Green and the focal point. When Francis Awsiter – a man of very high position in London – took over in 1602, he was married to Jane Horseman and the union produced four children. Richard, the only son, succeeded his father in 1624.

Unfortunately, this was a somewhat sketchy period, and little has come to hand to enlarge upon the fact that Richard Awsiter died in 1640 and that his eldest son was under 21 years of age when he became Francis Awsiter II, Lord of the Manor. Detail does emerge that Francis was the largest landowner in the district with 425 acres. A census of the population of Southall then, in 1653, is given as 81. Francis II died in 1666 (the year of the plague) but there is no evidence that this was the cause of his demise.

His younger brother, Robert, became the fourth member of the family to take the title, and he married twice – first to Rose who died in 1661, and then to Margarett Awnsham of Heston. His second wife produced a son – born in 1665 – who took over on the death of his father in 1683, becoming Richard Awsiter II at the early age of 18 years. In 1705 Richard died without issue and the Manor passed into the hands of his brother, Robert.

Again little is known of Robert Awsiter II except that he was married and had two children, both of whom died in infancy. The last member of the family to assume the title was John Awsiter, but the relationship to his predecessors is uncertain apart from the fact that he had nine children, but only one survived infancy.

A memorial tablet in Norwood Church describes John as a Doctor of Medicine, and during the Regency it is claimed that he discovered the beneficial effects of sea-water, thus bringing into prominence such places as Brighton. John died in 1756 and the Manor passed to his son, Thomas, who immediately sold the manorial rights. The manor, however, remained with the family until after Thomas died in 1801, and it was not until 1821 that it finally was sold and changed hands being bought by William Welch. The new owner was no stranger to the district, having acquired the lease of Southall market from the Earl of Jersey in 1801 and rebuilding it at a cost of £1,277.6.4. William Welch restored the Manor House extensively, probably adding the new West wing and Clock Tower – a part demolished for road widening after the First World War.

The next occupant, William Thomas, took up residence in 1879. He was a corset manufacturer of Cheapside and was instrumental in introduction the lock-stitch sewing machine into this country in 1847. The Thomas family became renowned for its lavish entertainment, and one can read of occasions when some of the foremost artistes of the day attended to entertain.

At the turn of the century it was in the hands of a Mr. Scarisbrick who had bought it from a famous surgeon, John Howard Mummery, who had held it for only three years. Mr. Scarisbrick left the Manor House in 1912, when it was placed in the hands of agents for sale. It was bought by the Council in 1913 for the sum of £6,100, and remained with them throughout two World Wars. In 1970 it was leased to the Chamber of Commerce at a nominal rent.

In the Edwardian period the house was partially hidden from the road by trees and iron railings. The grounds had a high brick wall and wooden entrance gates which enclosed three cottages each of which had front gardens.

Norwood

The Manor of Norwood has always been closely connected with the development of Southall. In the 12th century a chapel was established which was attached to the Parish Church of Hesa (Hayes). The building of the church in Norwood was largely due to Archbishop Chicheley in 1439. With outer walls of flint the porch is 15th century. Restorations took place in 1824, 1864 and 1896. The wooden belfry has been removed and the small Breck and Flint Western Tower erected. The belfry contained six bells originally.

Possibly the outbreak of the plague, and subsequent fire in London, had some influence on the fact that several well-known merchants had houses built on the outskirts, and many chose Norwood. Elisha Biscoe built and occupied Norwood Hall in 1765, also founding the Biscoe School. He was a great benefactor of Norwood

Church and contributed generously towards the cost of building the Old Rectory. Norwood Court was built by a Mr Henry Dodds – again a generous man in the area – who died in 1843.

The Plough public house dates back to the 14th century and had a rateable value in 1821 of £16 per year. It retains its old world appearance and boasts of a line of established licencees like the Dean family who lived there for over 70 years.

The Green at Norwood was originally 11 acres and had a pond. Sadly, due to neglect the pond had to be filled in, and road widening in 1930 reduced the acreage to 10. Famed for its avenue of great elms these fell victims to Dutch elm disease and had to be destroyed in 1977.

Between the green and the bridge at Norwood is an area known as Frogmore Green. Here, in 1688, four almshouses were built specifically for certain poor widows who each received six shillings weekly. Records show three farms in the district – Old Court Farm, Manor Farm and Alleyn Park.

Early Industrial Growth in Southall

Three factors materially contributed to the early prosperity of the town – its brick industry, the coming of the canal and the coming of the railway. In the 17th century it was discovered how good the local earth was for brick-making, and the *Stock* brick became rapidly a marketable product. Firms were established, and the district soon became encircled with brickfields and kilns, giving employment to many young men who were often exploited by their masters.

Most of the bosses build rows of small cottages for some of their employees. Of very low standard, these were more of an advantage to the masters as such dwellings ensured that the men were always on hand to attend to the kilns. With many of the brickfields producing, individually, up to eight million bricks in one year, brickmasters soon became wealthy people. The well-endowed families like the Reeds, Cullis, Hammonds, Watsons, Strouds, Newells and Brarveys became household names. At least the commodity they produced was of good quality, being used in the building of countless homes and many famous properties in and around London. In 1890 the price ranged from £1 for 250, delivered!

In 1792 *The Grand Junction Canal Company* was launched in Birmingham. Statutory notices were published for the canal to run from Braunston via Berkhampsted, Watford, Ruislip, Southall, and Hanwell to the Thames at Brentford. The canal dimensions were to be 42 ft wide at top; bottom 28ft; and depth 4.5 ft. The locks 15 ft wide and 86 ft long.

Work started at both ends in May, 1793, with 370 men on the payroll, this gradually increasing to 800. Their pay ranged from two shillings a day in accordance with their grade. The men worked in deplorable conditions, most of the digging being done manually, with horse and wagon transport. All the lock gates were made by hand on site.

The canal opened from Brentford to Uxbridge on Monday, 3rd November, 1794, and the Paddington branch from Bulls Bridge on 10 July, 1801. Water came from the Colne and Ouse. The canal virtually turned Southall into an island, with bridges built at Windmill Lane, Norwood Road; Old Oak Bridge, Western Road; Hayes Bridge and Northolt Bridge.

Docks were opened up to serve mainly the several brickmaking establishments in the area, but, as new firms developed in the locality, they too, found the canal a suitable means to transport their wares. The longboats (or barges) were all horse-drawn, generally being led by hand along the towpath.

To serve this traffic several small beer-houses came into being within the immediate vicinity. The Prince of *Wales* – at the end of Havelock Road; the King's Head – side of towpath where the *Junction Arms* is now situated; the *Blue Boar* near Bull's Bridge; and the *Hambrough Tavern* near Hayes Bridge. *The White Lion*, originally along the canal side was transferred to the corner of White Street and the Gas Factory Strait.

Although the canal system made the transportation of bricks and other goods simple and more economic, the passenger and postal services still had no alternative but use the stagecoach along the London-Oxford and London-Bath roads. The Uxbridge Road through Southall left much to be desired as far as condition was concerned, and the coming of the railway from Paddington must have been eagerly anticipated.

Isambard Kingdom Brunel's Great Western Railway came to the town in 1839, delayed by the building of the Wharncliffe Viaduct. The construction of this feat of engineering was by far the largest piece of work along the initial section of the line between London and Maidenhead. The contract, let on 1 November, 1835, took about 18 months to complete.

Crossing the Brent Valley proved to be the problem as the extremely soft clay would not bear the weight of a conventional pier construction. Brunel, therefore, adopted the novel – and then unique – solution of making the piers both hollow and slightly pyramidal. In addition he diverted the river into its present brick inverted arch.

The viaduct which is 300 yards long and 65 feet high, has arches of approximately 70 feet span. It was originally constructed for double broad gauge track, each elliptical arch being slightly different. The narrow gauge arches were added in 1877, when the railway was quadrupled.

The line through Southall in essence cut the place into two. It crossed the lane leading from the London-Oxford Road to Southall Green (then called Green Lane), with a level-crossing at first, then later, this was rectified by the installation of a station bridge in 1859. This intrusion tended to divide the community into two also – those who lived on the south side, 'over the Green' and those on the north side, 'over the other side' or later, 'over the trams'.

The year 1859 also saw the opening of the branch line to Brentford, built in order to allow goods traffic to avoid road congestion to the London Docks, and also afford access for those who wished to shop in the old market town of Brentford. Originally known as the Brentford and Great Western Junction, it was the last broad gauge track opened during the lifetime of Brunel. To negotiate the canal and road bridge over, Brunel conceived the plan of taking the railway under both, with the addition of a further bridge at Norwood (Tentelow Lane) resulting in what has become widely known as the *Three Bridges* – yet another engineering masterpiece.

On its journey through Southall, the railway contravened two right of ways – to the east of the station where the church path between the Southall and Norwood churches had been cut, and to the west of the station where an ancient footpath which led from the green and through the gas works had been severed. The first error was soon rectified by the building of a footbridge, but the second oversight was not righted until 1885, and only then flagrant trespassing of the railway property and prosecution saw justice done, and a subway tunnel being constructed at a cost of £300.

The coming of the railway meant the demise of the stagecoach, and the growth of industry in the area. Railway sidings allowed prospective businesses to more easily receive raw materials and transport manufactured goods. The first to exploit this new prospect was the Brentford Gas Company, who in 1868, bought 17.5 acres of land for £6,325 between the Paddington branch of the Grand Junction Canal and the Great Western Railway west of the station.

On 4 December, 1869 the first gas was produced. The first gasholder had a capacity of 480,000 cubic feet. In 1887 another 13 acres of land were purchased, and most of the houses in the district were being installed with gas lighting. Indeed, the gas industry was still expanding fifty years later when in 1929-30 the huge waterless German designed gasholder – now an accepted landmark- was built, its construction watched daily by the author.

In 1893, a site of 68 acres adjacent to the railway, near the station, was purchased, and a start made on what was to become the largest margarine works in the world, Otto Monsteds. The first contract went to the Southall firm of A. & B. Hanson worth £300,000. A private road was made and a railway siding constructed, entailing the extension of the footbridge by 20 yards. The factory was formally opened by the Earl of Jersey on 20 March, 1895.

Housing and Education

The canal did nothing to increase the population of the area, then still known as Southwould, immediately. It was only around 800 in 1800 and but 2,300 in 1840 – due in no small measure to the building of the Hanwell Asylum as this institution came within the Southall/Norwood boundary, and thus the staff living in, and patients, were included in that total.

Whilst the initial bargee expertise came from the Midlands, the people tended to be nomadic, and few families, settled in Southall – as it had now become known – this was not so when it came to the railway. At first, train drivers and fireman settled around the departure and destination points – like at Swindon, Reading, and Paddington. Gradually, as the service developed and it was a simple exercise to commute daily, families began to filter into the areas around the suburban stations. A growing need to maintain the line also demanded a localised workforce, so it is not surprising to find the population creeping up to 4,470 by 1860; 6,650 by 1880 and 8,500 by 1890.

With the town literally parting at the seams, an urgent housing programme was needed. This came at the close of the 19th century and continued until start of the First World War. One has only to compare the maps of Ordnance Survey for the years 1894-6 and 1914, to appreciate this great change.

South of the railway, by 1914, Kingston Road had been completed; Osterley Park Road, Church Avenue, Hartington Road, Queen's Road, Gladstone Road, Featherstone Road, and Dudley Road had been built, whilst a whole complex had opened up around the Adelaide Road area. North of the railway a similar picture can be seen – Lady Margaret Road, Shackleton Road, Alexandra Avenue, Northcote Avenue and Saxon Gardens had become evident on the north of the main road; on the south side, Herbert Road, Beechcroft Avenue, Oswald Road, Abbotts Road and others have been added.

This huge spate of building naturally attracted a workforce from far and wide. Carpenters, bricklayers, plumbers, tilers, painters and gas fitters, – mainly from London – descended on Southall and sought lodgings; a certain percentage eventually bringing their families and setting up homes in the district.

As was the case in many places, the Church had a hand in early education. In 1837, a local benefactor, a Mr. Dodds, connected with St. John's Church, donated enough money to build a school in Southall Green facing Western Road, which took up to 150 pupils.

Around 1851, rather strangely located to the north where mainly brickfields prevailed, North Road Mixed School was built to take 200 pupils. Drawing most of its children from Southall Green, the journey must have been arduous on a winter's day. A house was built for the first headmaster next to the school. Some 20 years later another school was built – Norwood Bridge School – for girls and infants who had to pay one penny a week. Gradually enlarged, it was able to take up to 350 in 1886. Conditions at the school seem to have been poor, illness both with staff and pupils being often reported. In 1894 it was changed to infants only.

In 1858, in South Road, a school which catered for orphans (Marylebone School) was built, standing in its own grounds. Financed by the Catholic Church it did fine work among the poor and destitute children in London.

These early schools in no way could take the upsurge of population to come at the turn of the century. In 1891, the first Featherstone Road School was built on a site costing £175. North Road Infants' School came in 1892, and Dudley Road School – built 1897 on a site costing £200 – was open to educate the girls of the district only. During this last decade two private schools opened Southall High School and a Boarding School in Norwood Green.

In 1901 the large Featherstone Boys' School was built for 500 boys. Mr. Dunn became its first headmaster, and when he retired in 1904, Mr. West took over and was in charge until 1932. Four more schools followed – Clifton Road School in 1904, built to hold 800 pupils; Talbot Road School in 1907; Southall County School built in 1906-7 (which took only three free scholarship pupils from each of the senior schools, and the rest had to pay): Tudor Road School also in 1906-7, built to take 250 children. Outside the immediate parish, in 1854, St. Mary's Orphanage, North Hyde School – previously a military barracks – had been taken over to accommodate 600 boys.

At War

The Boer War did little to disturb the normal life of Southall. The main effect it had, if any, was on the young men of the area who were largely working in the brickfields. In their case it was instrumental in giving them a career which they never would have had in the brick-making industry. When the war ended a large number of local soldiers chose to sign on for continued service rather than return to civilian life.

The Great War, on the other hand, affected nearly every family in Southall and Norwood, and caused much hardship for those left behind. The actual Declaration of War – at 4 p.m. on 4 August 1914 – caught everyone by surprise, being a Bank Holiday.

Gradually the factories changed over and became part of the war effort. Abbotts making ammunition boxes and hospital furniture, and firms like Ticklers and Kearley and Tonge gaining contracts to supply their various products. Women began to replace men – especially on munition work at Hayes.

The 'Gazette' offices in the High Street and King Street were used as centres for recruiting, and naturally, most enrolled into the Middlesex Regiment. In less than two months, sadly, some 80% were to be reported killed, wounded or missing. Belgium refugees began to arrive and were housed in South Road, and a prisoner-of-war camp was set up for German servicemen at Osterley Park.

The wounded were catered for in Marylebone School, where an Australian hospital was set up, and the Maypole Institute, which was turned into a military hospital run by VAD nurses. When the latter closed in 1919 it had treated some 3,300 patients, of which some 2,500 had come from the trenches in France. On 23 November 1916, King George and Queen Mary paid the hospital a visit – at that time 102 patients were being treated.

After the war King and Hutchings published a Roll of Honour which recorded details of all Southall men who had died in the war, and in due course, every school and church in the town commemorated those scholars and members who had made the supreme sacrifice, by a plaque or tablet.

Rumblings of the Second World War came to Southall in 1938 with the issuing of civilian respirators to every householder in the district. At nearby Heston Airport, Neville Chamberlain had landed from Munich bearing the famous agreement, which did little more than stave off the war for a while.

When war did eventually break out on 3 September 1939, Southall, because of its huge gasholder, was thought to be vulnerable to bombing. Actually, it turned out to be more of a landmark for German air attacks rather than a target.

Civil Defence Services were immediately active with exercises. The Ambulance Section was based at The Manor House, whilst the Rescue and Casualty Services were housed in the Council Depot at Endsleigh Road.

In contrast with many London areas, Southall came out of the war with but little damage. Of the bombs that did drop on the town, its schools were the first to suffer. On 28 September 1940 North Road School was damaged, closing it for six weeks. On 15 October 1940 an outside shelter at Tudor Road School was hit. There were no casualties in either case.

In 1941 bombs dropped on Cambridge Road and also destroyed Woolworths in the High Street. There were several daylight raids – one of a landmine causing wide damage and casualties at the top of Lady Margaret Road. In a night raid, a row of shops was demolished in Tentelow Lane, Norwood Green.

In 1944 Southall first experienced flying bombs. On a Sunday afternoon in June of that year, one fell and destroyed the old Rectory at Norwood. Another, on 29 August 1944, destroyed a number of houses in Adelaide Road. Bombs also dropped on the retort house at the Gas Works. Sadly, two of our own 'planes came down – a Wellington bomber crashing in the Gas Works' field and a Spitfire inside the gates of the factory itself.

Conscription, which had been enforced from the start, gradually drew men and women from their occupations, and it was only the unfit and more elderly who escaped some form of military service. Seven flying bombs in total fell on Southall, killing two people and injuring 80. The damage to houses was great in comparison, 3,482 properties needing attention.

Commerce

Until the turn of the century Southallians did their main shopping in Brentford, but with the coming of more housing, and industrialisation, naturally commerce followed suit. Tradesmen were quick to appreciate the potential of the somewhat scattered young town with a population of around 10,000.

The chief shopping area was fast growing on the southern side, with a few shops in the High Street. Apart from this the district largely comprised of cornfields and brickfields. Then came the Edwardian era, and the formation of an association which eventually became a Chamber of Commerce.

This move was triggered off by the Coronation of King Edward VII, when the Establishment proclaimed the day – Saturday 9 August 1902 – a Bank Holiday, naturally an inconvenient time for the tradespeople to close their shops, with men being paid their wages on Friday night or Saturday mid-day.

A meeting of fellow-tradesmen was called and 28 turned up for discussion, when it was finally resolved to close all shops on the required day, but open all day on the previous Wednesday. With that part of the proceedings concluded, it was then proposed that a local Tradesmen's Association be formed. Mr. Beckett was voted to the Chair and in due course became the first president.

The new organisation became most active in the town, drawing the attention of particular authorities to matters of importance – both to residents and shopkeepers – like the condition of the roads; the lack of sweeping and control of dust; the saving of rates and the collection of letters (five collections and deliveries a day being normal, with the last at 9 p.m. – an extension to this being requested at 11 p.m. when shops closed).

As the population increased so did the shopping facilities, and by 1908 over 100 members had joined, some of which became candidates and eventually served on the District Council. In 1912 the name of the organisation was changed to Southall-Norwood Chamber of Commerce.

During the First World War most of the routine work was dropped in favour of the war effort. Shops closed as their owners were called up. Members of the Chamber did excellent work by sitting on various committees. After the war membership continued to grow, and by 1923, when the Chamber celebrated its 21st birthday, it was firmly established. The life of Southall has benefitted from its work ever since. The Chamber's greater achievement must be the saving of The Manor House, because without the prompt action of its members in negotiating the tenancy of this grand old place as the Chamber's headquarters in 1970, this 16th century edifice might not be there today.

ROOTS AND RELIGION

Souvenir card given to the author's parents after their wedding. Rev. Roberts died 11 July 1934. c.1910.
The old parish church of St. John's in Southall Green was built in 1837 and consecrated the next year, the first
vicar being Rev. F. Hewson. By 1910 it had become too small for its growing congregation.

NEW PARISH CHURCH OF ST. JOHN, SOUTHALL.

EXTERIOR.

Picture postcard published to celebrate the new church opening showing St. John's Church, Southall, its exterior and interior aspects. c.1910. The new St. John's Church was built on the land where once Elmfield House stood. Costing £8,000 and seating 750, the building was consecrated by the Bishop of London on 26 October 1910.

A typical Southall Green scene of the period around 1914.· Looking north towards the station, the parade of shops in the right includes Charleworth's Studios – a venue for many of the locals wishing to preserve family portraits. Note the soldiers (one with kit-bag) making their way to the trains.

Norwood Church, Southall

Largely with the help of Archbishop Chichelely, St. Mary the Virgin Church at Norwood Green, was built in 1430, the parish then including Southall Green. Seating 280, its registers date from: baptisms 1654; marriages 1655; and burials 1659. The churchyard closed for burials in 1883.

HOLY TRINITY CHURCH, SOUTHALL

Built on a parcel of land at Park View road and High Street, Holy Trinity Church was consecrated by the Bishop of London in 1890, replacing one made of corrugated iron which had been on loan for 18 years. The Rev. Henry Mills was the incumbent at the time. He died on 25 April 1917.

SOUTH ROAD, SOUTHALL

Left, the newly opened King's Hall after work had been completed. c. 1916.

Published by John King, Printer & Stationer, Southall

Baptist Chapel, Southall

The Baptist Church, although active for some years in Southall previously, did not have its own church until 1889. Situated at the corner of St. John's Road and Western Road, it was rebuilt in 1901 since when side halls have been added.

Southall—Norwood Cemetery.

A workman trims the grass verge in the old Southall Cemetery in Havelock Road. Although the cemetery was opening after Norwood Churchyard closed in 1883, the chapel was not built until 1896. c.1905.

Robinson's Flour mill beside the canal as it appeared in 1903. After being destroyed by fire in 1912 the site was taken over by the Haig family who set up a picture framing works.

SOUTHALL.—STATION FROM FOOTBRIDGE

The railway came to Southall in 1839. The line was first laid with wide (or broad) track. At that time only a level crossing was provided to allow Green Lane traffic to pass from one part of the town to the other. Taken from the station footbridge looking west, this fine animated railway scene takes in the main, local and branch lines. In the background can be seen the distinctive castle-like shape of the water tower. c.1905.

Bird's-Eye View from Water Tower, Southall.

A bird's eye view of the railway complex taken from the Water Tower west of the station in 1905. The panoramic setting shows the main line heading off toward Paddington, whilst the branch line forks right to Brentford.

THE THREE BRIDGES, SOUTHALL.

The Three Bridges, built to facilitate the Brentford branch line from Southall, is a much-photographed subject.
In its early days it became known as The Wonderful Bridge. c.1940.

Southall Station & Bridge.

A lonely horse-drawn cart and driver negotiates the bridge at Southall station. Looking north, at the bottom of the hill, can be seen *The Railway Hotel.* c.1926.

With the coming of the Great Western railway, many factories began to make themselves evident, with their own sidings. T.G. Tickler's jam factory, to the west of the station, became a thriving enterprise. Nearby came the Victor Tyre Company and Scott's Emulsion. c.1910.

Otto Monsted Margarine Works set up before the turn of the century, employed a large number of Southall people. The Company wound up around 1925, causing a deal of unemployment in the town. A picture of the works at the bottom of Bridge Road (then Margarine Road), including the newly-built Club and Institute.

15

PACKING ROOM, OTTO MONSTED, LTD., SOUTHALL WORKS.

The firm, ever-mindful to impress their customers on hygiene in the works, produced this trade card showing the packing room. Details on the reverse noted the modern conditions under which the staff worked in the 'twenties.

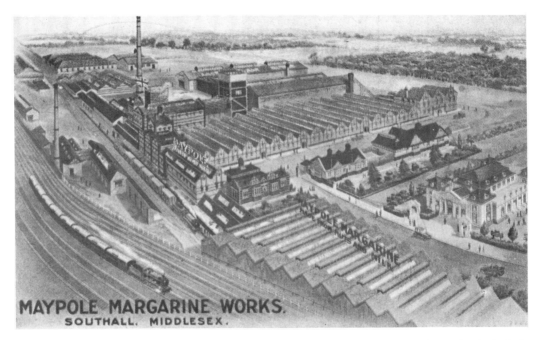

A fine trade card widely used showed the whole Maypole complex. The artist, however, has omitted to include the footbridge over the railway.

A solitary horse plods its way along the towpath of the canal, pulling a couple of barges. This picture, taken c.1905, gives some indication of the small industrial establishments that set up in business along the waterway.

An aerial view of Southall (south of the railway) in 1927. Centrally: the war memorial, and opposite, *The Romans* with a fair in its grounds; left: *The Manor House* and grounds; top right: the gaswork's cricket field.

HOUSING AND EDUCATION

PUBLIC LIBRARY & OSTERLEY PARK ROAD, SOUTHALL.

Built at the turn of the century, Osterley Park Road catered for some of the town's elite – doctors, builders and business men – apart from a private school. The better class roads were generally distinguished by the planting of trees.

Kingston Road, a strange mixture of better class on one side and lesser on the other, is seen from the Church Path and looking toward The Green. The road clearly shows where tradesmen have turned their vehicles at the cul-de-sac.

South Road looking north to the town hall distant. In the early 1900's the majority of the building was contained on the right side, whilst, on the left, a close-boarded fence masked the Marylebone School.

A delivery cart trundles up Northcote Avenue in 1909 while, in the distance, the newly-built *Northcote Arms* stands resplendent, under the landlordship of Mr. Gerrard. The house at that time could be rented for 12s 6d per week.

Abbotts Road, named after the Abbott family who came to Southall in 1876 and started up a business next to the town hall as joiners and polishers. Charles Abbott started the fire service and later, in 1936, C.J. Abbott became Deputy Charter Mayor. c.1918.

Tudor Road – leading north from the Uxbridge Road – houses the school by that name. The school, like the road, was built around 1906-7 to take 250 pupils. It had gas lighting until 1952.

Avenue Road, Southall

The tree-lined Avenue Road is seen with buildings on the west side only. The authorities, intent on keeping the footpath intact as a church path, would not allow houses to be built on the east side. c.1905.

Lady Margaret Road, which only went as far as Shackleton Road until 1925, was a fairly high-class neighbourhood. Tree-lined; it housed people like school teachers and heads; builders and estate agents/ owners.

A group of children make their way to school on a bright summer morning, some clutching their hoops; built in 1851, the North Road Mixed School accommodated 200 pupils. In 1894 Mr. Wilson, who was headmaster, lived with his wife in a schoolhouse next door. His salary – £192 per annum. c.1905.

The Southall County School in Villiers Road was built in 1906/7 with Mr. Pollett as its first headmaster. For many years the school authorities restricted its free scholarships to only three pupils from each elementary school.

Western Road Girls' School, built in 1911 on land purchased in 1896, because of its unusual shape on plan,
soon became known as *The Aeroplane School.* c.1912.

A grocery van delivers while children loiter. Clifton Road School, built around 1903/4 originally catered for 800 pupils. The staff and scholars were transferred from Norwood Bridge School. c.1910.

Featherstone Road, Infant's & Boys School Southall.

A mother takes her child to school while two ancient residents pause to pass the time of day outside the gate. Featherstone Road School – built for 500 boys in 1901 – added to an earlier section (nearer camera), which then became the Infants' school. c.1907.

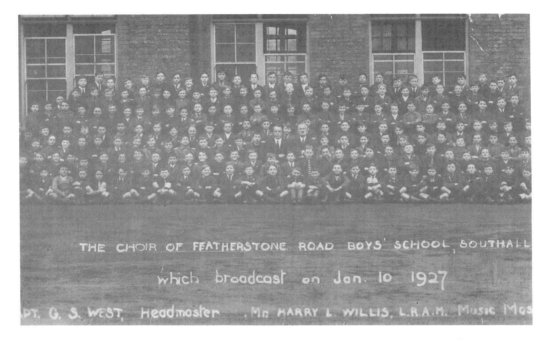

THE CHOIR OF FEATHERSTONE ROAD BOYS' SCHOOL, SOUTHALL
which broadcast on Jan. 10 1927
PT. G. S. WEST, Headmaster , Mr HARRY L WILLIS, L.R.A.M. Music Mas

A red-letter day for Featherstone Road schoolboys was when their choir was chosen to be the first elementary school to broadcast. The performance took place at The King's Hall before an audience of 1,200. The items included sea shanties, part and unison songs – all appreciated by a wide listening audience. The author appears in the photograph.

Dudley Road Girls' School, Southall.

Dudley Road Girls' School was built in 1897, on a site costing £200. Here classes assemble in the playground with their teachers. One can imagine with what care pinafores were laundered beforehand. c.1905.

A local street trader pauses in delivering some produce to householders in Avenue Road. This view (looking north to the High Street), shows how the church path (right), has been left untouched with the road constructed alongside. c.1905.

Waltham Road around 1912. To the right is the yard of H. Imhoff, estate agent, who was responsible for a lot of properties in Southall during the building programme pre-1914.

St John's Road (looking towards Featherstone Road) as seen around 1910. In the distance is Featherstone Terrace – unkindly called 'Bug Alley' – with Barnes, the drapers, at the corner. In due course this became a general stores.

The Manor House, Southall.

The long history of *The Manor House* in Southall Green makes this the most photographed and written about building in the town. Its future has been in doubt at times, but now it is in the protective hands of the Chamber of Commerce. A John King picture postcard, postally used in 1906.

Geo. Lowe & Co., estate agents, put *The Manor House* up for sale in 1912 for the freehold price of £5,000 which included the grounds and outbuildings. The sale notice makes interesting reading and the detail gives a comprehensive picture of the property. It was eventually bought by the Council for £6,100.

At home, in the town, certain premises were being utilised as make-shift centres for the wounded. Ivy-clad Marylebone School in South Road was soon pressed into service as a Military Hospital for Australian soldiers.

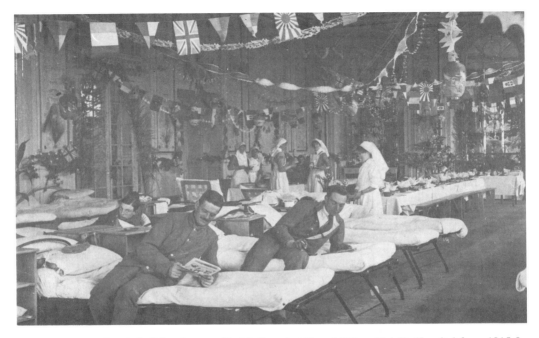

The Maypole Institute's building became No.11 Gen. Auxiliary Military V.A.D. Hospital from 1915-9, handling 3,000 patients of which 2,500 came from the trenches in France. A Christmas scene in Ward III in 1918.

Nº809. TENNIS COURT.
AUXILIARY MILITARY V.A.D. HOSPITAL, SOUTHALL.

Wounded servicemen play tennis on the Maypole courts. King George V and Queen Mary visited the hospital on 23 November, 1916. The site of the tennis courts is now housing *The Limes* home. c.1918.

War Memorial & Manor House, Southall.   Photo Surveys.

War memorials sprang up after the conflict in many schools and churches. The town's tribute – dedicated on 8 April, 1922, by the Hon. Sydney Peel, M.P. – stands on the site of the old Manor House cottages. The adding of 1939-45 dates this picture as c.1949.

Crowds thronged to see the unveiling of the Featherstone Road School Monument Memorial by Field Marshal Sir Wm. Robertson on 16 February, 1921. The school lost two teachers and 226 old boys in the hostilities.

The peace which followed the war saw several yearly demonstrations of remembrance. Here in the Manor House grounds representatives of the British Legion (Mens' and Womens' Sections) and the Old Contemptibles, parade for an Armistice service. c.1934. Extreme left is Capt.J.J.Bridges, Chairman of the Southall Branch of the Old Contemptibles.

Rumblings of the Second World War brought together the town's voluntary organisations. Almost first in the field were the St. John Ambulance Nursing Division. This group is pictured outside their H/Q at *The Grange* in the Green. c.1939.

When the Casualty Services came into being many joined from the St. John and Red Cross locally. This early group, stationed in the Council Depot in Endsleigh Road, had still to be issued with their uniforms. c.1939.

A stretcher party ready for action in 1940. A section of the Casualty and Rescue Services, each comprised of a driver and four men. The author is pictured as leader wearing a white helmet.

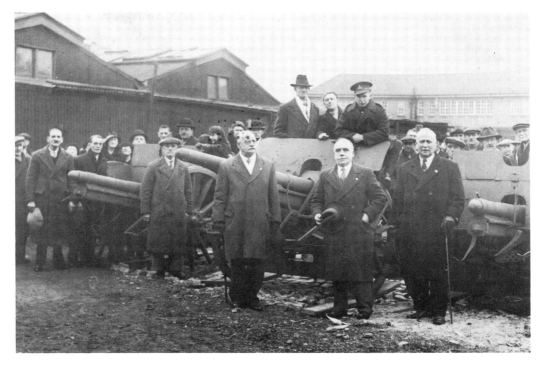

When the Australian Hospital, based at Marylebone School, finally closed in 1919, the Australian Government as a token of friendship handed over some German guns to the town. In 1939, these were donated to help the war effort. Picture taken outside the old British Legion.

COMMERCE

The Old Smithy. 1902
now New Broadway. Southall.

A pleasant rural spot at the corner of South Road/High Street at the turn of the century, Leggatt's Smithy and cottage opposite the *Three Horseshoes* was demolished in 1902 to make way for progress. The smithy saw its heyday at the time when horse traffic along the Uxbridge Road brought business.

H. J. BUTLER & Co's New Tailoring Premises,

THE BROADWAY, SOUTHALL.

(late LEGGETT'S FORGE.)

The New Corner.

The Old Corner.

H.J.Butler's were not slow in exploiting their new position when Leggatt's forge was pulled down. This trade card issued by the firm in 1903/4 compares the corner with that of the past.

The Broadway corner – now built up – looking west c.1914. Pedestrians loiter in a strangely quiet main road as a tram stops to pick up passengers.

The parade of shops ready in 1913 appears to be doing plenty of trade. Sainsbury's, quick to see the opportunies, have acquired a prime position, followed by Richardson's and Chamberlain's.

NEW PARADE, SOUTHALL.   No 2

Commerce began to stretch along the main road in the 'twenties. New Parade is here seen, looking west towards Hayes bridge.

Looking east along a deserted High Street. c.1907. The trams came to Southall in 1902 and turned round at Haddrell's corner. The town hall then had only a stone portico.

The town hall and Broadway, looking east, in 1920, towards Hanwell. The town hall was built in 1897 on land given by the Earl of Jersey. Opened by his wife on 8 November 1897, the building cost £9,000. By the time this picture was published a glass-canopied entrance had been added to the stone portico.

The Three Horseshoes on the corner of South Road (previously Green Lane), has seen many changes. This picture c.1910, gives one the image of a quiet town – a horse and cart waits patiently outside the shop of John King, stationer and prolific picture postcard publisher.

Looking north from Dagmar Road (left) in King Street c.1910. A hive of activity on a bright summer morning, but little sign of traffic. The existence of a pawnshop (left) is a clear indication of the poverty which prevailed in Southall in most families at the time.

King Street (looking north) in the early 'thirties. The row of shops (right) reaching from Church Avenue to Havelock Road, were built on the site of the old Vicarage. Still standing at the time, Welch's Folly (the wall around Featherstone Hall), is seen in the distance.

A thriving row of shops in the High Street. Outside the bank men gather, while in Durbin's shop a poster bills
Marie Lloyd at Shepherd's Bush Empire c.1910.

LONDON BOROUGH OF
EALING PUBLIC LIBRARIES
Postcard Series No. D4

OLD SOUTHALL - NORWOOD
Poplar Cottages   1905
(Corner of King Street and Norwood Road)

Produced by
Pamlin Prints
Croydon

Two local worthies discuss a mutual topic at the corner of King Street and Norwood Road in 1905. A row of
shops, built on this site afterwards, was pulled down in 1932 – now a car park.

KING STREET, SOUTHALL.

Formerly Denmark Terrace on the coronation of King Edward VII it changed to King Street. Our picture –
looking north from Regina Road junction – gives a fine example of the town's traders around 1903/4.

Another lovely animated view of King Street, looking north, with the main street a hive of activity. Left,
Children sit on the pavement in the sunshine while a nearby shop advertises railway excursions to the coast.
c.1905.

A later view of King Street with John King's shop prominent on the left. King, the Southall postcard pioneer, was responsible for most of the Edwardian views of the town. Right, the paper shop exhibits all the news and The Gem cinema titles on its many placards.

Bank buildings, at the corner of Featherstone Road and King Street, has always been a popular gossip place.
From the Co-op to St. John's Church Hall, most of the shops were run by the same proprietors for years. Who
can forget Madame Hancock, in the haberdashery shop – an eccentric but lovable lady. c.1905.

A group outside *The Havelock Arms* – probably picking today's winner – merge with shoppers in King Street c.1910. On the opposite corner, Western Road. The picture appears to be around 1910.

View of Southall Green in the early 'twentie. Right is *The Victory* public house – renamed from *The Duke of Prussia* in 1915 because of public indignation against Germany – and centre is the strange wall built by a Mr. Welch which bordered a private asylum all of which was pulled down in 1931 to make way for The Dominion Cinema and a row of shops.

The Green (looking south) c.1912. Two uniformed postmen (left) pass The Gem cinema (right) with its lurid forthcoming attractions. The Gem, built in 1910, was the first cinema in Southall – dubbed 'the fleapit' it was a cheap form of entertainment.

A group of schoolboys cross the road at the junction of King Street and Featherstone Road. Left is *The Duke of Prussia* (changed in 1915 to *The Victory*). The Co-op shop is on the right corner. c.1910.

King Street, Southall.

A policeman stands on duty at the junction of King Street and Western Road around 1908. Endicote's, the drapery shop on the corner, was completely destroyed by fire on 27 November 1914. A busy shopping scene looking south to the bank on the corner of Regina Road.

A group of children pose on the steps of the garden entrance to the Southall Recreation Ground. Backing the scene is Florence Road with its back additions, complete with washing hanging on lines. c.1915.

Children play around the bandstand in the recreation ground. In the background (right) can be seen houses in Western Road. c.1908.

Open Air SwimmingBath. Southall.

W.HA.596.

The open air swimming baths in the recreation grounds had been open around four years when this picture was taken in 1916. It was then quite primitive and needed Spartan-like bathers to brave the waters. A mere handful are seen taking the plunge almost fully dressed!

Some twenty years later the baths show signs of modernisation. An aeration plant has been added; cubicles have been altered and buildings to the front and side now give more facilities. c.1936.

Southall Park was purchased in 1901 by the Council. Originally a private asylum, run by Dr. Boyd, a disastrous fire in 1883 burnt town the house and caused the death of the doctor and six others. c.1912.

John King has turned an early card of the Golf Links into a Christmas card. This postcard – postally used in 1908 – shows the original club house and, in the distance, St. Mary's Church spire at Hanwell.

The Maypole Institute is pictured in 1920 back in civilian use after being used as a military hospital during the war. Shirt sleeves and straw hats seem to be the order of the day at this bowls match.

No park would be complete without its band. Several organisations possessed good ones which competed for the honour of playing. Our picture shows the British Legion Band c.1936 with dog mascot.

Winners of the Westminster Challenge Shield. 1910.

For decades the boys at St. Mary's School, North Hyde had a band worthy of the highest awards. Clad in their olive-green tunics and wearing bush-type hats, led by Mr.Dunn, bandmaster, they won many trophies. c.1912.

NORWOOD GREEN.

A delightfully rural scene at Norwood as a flour delivery is made to Birch's Bakery in 1912. A patient horse munches a bag of oats and a solitary dog trots across the road.

A later scene in 1917 over the Green at Norwood. Centrally can be seen the bakery which also was pressed into service as the post office.

Norwood Green, Southall.

Published by John King, Printer and Stationer, Southall

A 105/231

A local resident relaxes in the peaceful environment of Norwood Green and contemplates the pond. An early King postcard postally used in 1905.

PLOUGH INN, NORWOOD GREEN, SOUTHALL.

The Plough Inn claims to date back to 1349. This historic building at Norwood is Fuller, Smith and Turner's oldest public house. In our picture c.1900, children pose with the traditional wooden hoop, while a delivery cart possibly brings another consignment of the local brew.

Frogmore Green, Norwood, Southall.

Interested youngsters in a strangely deserted Norwood Road at Frogmore Green, gazed fixedly at the photographer of this scene. The inclusions of a vintage pram dates the period as c.1906.

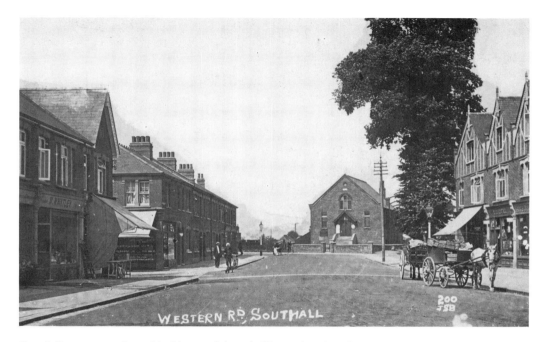

Two delivery carts wait outside this row of shops in Western Road. Left-Fowler's, the bakers, seem to be well stocked and open for business. The old Primitive Methodist Church stands in centre distance c.1916.

Looking west from Waltham Road, Western Road seem almost deserted, The S.P.Q.R. Stores, a popular hardware shop, and the rest of the parade, appear to be closed. c.1916.

LONDON BOROUGH OF
EALING PUBLIC LIBRARIES
Postcard Series No. D3

OLD SOUTHALL – NORWOOD
Fire Brigade outside the Town Hall c1900

Produced by
Pamlin Prints
Croydon

Southall's first fire engine. Mr. C. Abbott was the chief officer and pioneered the service in 1901. In due course it was established next to the town hall, costing £175. The firemen were nearly all Abbott's staff. Firemen – Messrs. Hasman, Ward, Strickland, Parslow, Foster, T. Smith and A. Smith.

Featherstone Road Boys' School football team 1930-1 when they won the Gosney Cup. Team – L to R back row: Palmer, Goodall, Davis, L to R mid row: Perry and Lipscombe, L to R front row: F.Marchant, Moore, G.Marchant, Cheal and Timberlake. Adults L to R: Mr. Foxell (teacher), Capt. West (headmaster), Mr.Huxtable (sportsmaster) and Mr. Smith (caretaker).

A jolly gathering of old soldiers take to the charabancs for an outing. Taken in the drive leading to the old British Legion Club, with Featherstone Hall in the background. c.1926-7.

Looking south down South Road. c.1908. An early morning scene showing a remarkably traffic free main
road with shoppers with prams, school-children and commuters evident.

This c.1905 postally used card, includes part of the little Sunday School and the side of the Marylebone School (left). Amongst those gathered, two postmen have got themselves in on the act.

POST OFFICE, SOUTHALL

The camera takes a slightly different view, with the cinema at the corner of Beaconsfield Road, exhibiting some lurid placards.

A solitary roadsweeper cleans the gutters in Featherstone Road. In the centre distance can be seen the Drill Hall, built in 1901, which housed a Middlesex Regiment Territorial Company. c.1916.

South Road, Southall.

Proceeding northwards from The Green, this c.1908 picture takes in the residence known as *The Chestnuts* – eventually to become Southall/Norwood Hospital. Osterley Park Road leads off right.

SOUTH ROAD SOUTHALL

A later view, c.1913, from almost the same position, shows clearly the amount of road widening which had taken place. The road condition, though, had not changed!

95

A scene of much animation and intense interest is obvious on the occasion of the laying of the first gas main across the Grand Union Canal, next to the old Wolf Bridge in the 1880's. In the background is Robinson's Flour Mill (burnt down in 1912) and the sewer pipe along the bridge.

Good morning! Reverend
MacDonald greets Doctor
MacDonald as they cycle along
Norwood Road past the Green.
Rev. MacDonald was the
incumbent at St. Mary's and
Dr. MacDonald was a
practitioner in Southall. c.1903.

A scene at the opening of Southall/Norwood Public library, built on a plot of land in Osterley Park Road. The ceremony was carried out by Mrs. Bigwood in 1905 and was attended by many dignatories, and apparently the recently formed fire brigade.

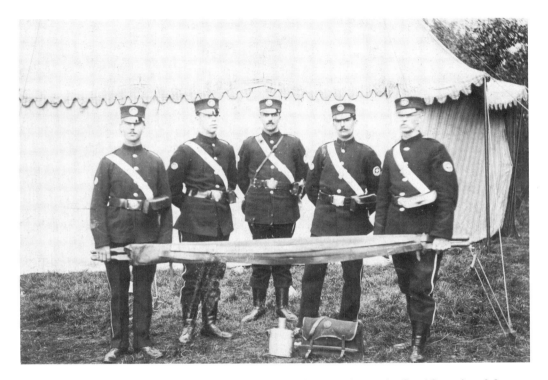

Members of the (Southall Section) No.44 West London Division, on duty at the Good Samaritan & League of Mercy Garden Fete, held in the grounds of South Lodge in The Green, on August Bank Holiday 1909. L to R: H.Vale, R.W. Day, M.Archer, J.E.Taylor and W.Archer.

A constable stands on duty outside Norwood Green Police Station c.1900. The station, built in 1890, had been originally sited for Adelaide Road, but police preference for Norwood prevailed.

A group of locals pose for the photographer in front of *The Wolf Inn* around 1890. The publican, E. Daniel, is not immediately seen, but tankards of Clutterbuck's ale or porter are evident.

Cricket on the Green at Norwood. c.1933. The cricket club, formed in 1872, The team, originally made up of a local gentry, has always been a force to be reckoned with in the area. In the background can be seen (left) Norwood Rectory – destroyed by a flying bomb in WWII, and (right) the 'pepper-pot' toilet – a quaint feature of the Green for many years.

Peaked caps, straw hats, bowlers, trilbys and some musical accompaniment – plus button-holes – much to the fore at this pub outing of the old *North Star* in the palmy days between the wars.

In the bar of the old British Legion, Mr. Bousfield, the president, has a pipe and a quiet drink while trade is slack. c.1938.

John King, in following the pattern of most picture postcard publishers, produced this 'Peeps round Southall & District' card. Covering the Three Bridges, the railway station, Top Lock, Norwood Pond and South Road, we are given a glimpse of the town c.1905.

The Red Lion Hotel, here is seen boasting of its 'Celebrated stout and ales' as supplied by Whitbread's. Opposite, a notice on a lamp standard reads `Electric Cars stop here by request'. c.1910.

The Sanatorium,
Mount Pleasant, Southall.

As with many London suburbs, Southall had its share of under-nourished people. Tuberculosis, prevalent in the late Victorian era, was treated in The Sanatorium at Mount Pleasant. Previously a fever hospital, the siting of it speaks well for the local air! c.1912.

Hanwell Mental Hospital seen from the air. Built 1833 by French prisoners-of-war, the staff and patients have always been included in the Southall population figures. Almost a self-supporting establishment, the Asylum had its own bakery, tailor's shop, bootshop, farm and church. c.1939.

Pictures of the Water Splash at North Hyde are rare. Here we see a group of youngsters getting in on the action, around 1908. The brook, always when in flood, was a hazard for carts, but was simply crossed by a footbridge.

The Working Men's Club, Southall

The Chestnuts taking its name from the large horse-chestnut tree outside – was taken over by The Working Men's Club on 8 September 1906. Here, some of its 350 members are pictured in the entrance, while others get in on the scene from the windows. In 1935 it became Southall Norwood Hospital.

Manor Parade, Southall.

A c.1950 picture of Manor Parade still portrays The Green as a sleepy backwater town. *The Romans* (left) and Manor cottages (right) were replaced twenty years previously to make a wider thoroughfare.

Platt's Stores, King Street, 1903. Delivery traps, shop assistants, and customers, line up in front of a prime display of what the Southall housewife would be buying for that day's table. The prominence of rabbit meat demonstrates the poorness of the neighbourhood.